240

Inspirational

Quotes

On Humility

240 Inspirational Quotes On Humility

Quotes That Lead To Humility

Rev. Fr. Peter Obinna Umekwe

To order additional copies of this book, contact:
Xlibris Corporation
1-888-795-4274
www.Xlibris.com
Orders@Xlibris.com
69043

Contents

Dedication

This book is dedicated to Monsignor Fortunatus Nwachukwu, Head of Protocol at the Vatican Secretariat of State Rome, in gratitude for his kindness to me and in appreciation of his humble attitude to life.

ACKNOWLEDGEMENTS

SPECIAL THANKS TO God Almighty, without whose inspiration this book would have remained an unrealized dream. To my parents and family members whose love has been a source of great strength to me. To my Bishops, home and abroad, whose paternal support and encouragement I have been privileged to enjoy.

To Dee Chukwuma Innocent Enyiorji and his family for their love and fellowship. To Mr. and Mrs. Loius Ubah and family for their kindness to me. To Mama Monica Asomugha for her prayers and help. To Mrs Regina Amankulor for her encouragement and benevolence. To Martin Ekpe and his family for their goodness to me. To Rev. Sr. Vitalis Chigbu for her thoughtfulness and kindness.

To Monsignor Fortunatus Nwachukwu, Fathers Pius Kii, Ikechukwu Ikeocha, Callistus Nwachukwu, Felix Alaribe, Leo Ogbonna, Reginald Nwauzo, Charles Nnabuife, Isaac Erondu, Fabian Nwokorie, Dominic Agbara, Emmanuel Chikezie, Desmond Chilagoro, Thomas Obiatuegwu, Chidi Ekpendu and Paulus Njoku for sustaining me in trying times. To Fr. Chukwudi O. Callistus Onwere for agreeing to proofread this book, for his helpful suggestions, and for his well-written Foreword.

To my friends, Loyd Smith and his wife, Mary Beth. In one of our conversations, Mary Beth encouraged me to write a book because she felt uplifted by some of my ideas. I was so deeply motivated by her words that I started researching and writing. She and Loyd championed my continuing efforts. So this book yields its birth to the motivation and encouragement of these great friends.

To my Parish Council members and my beloved parishioners for their collaboration, hospitality, team-spirit, cooperation, and support in my ministry. To my friends, Jim and Pat Heintzelman for their hospitality, solidarity, straight-forwardness and humility. As a professor of English, Pat did a good job in proof-reading the manuscript and fine-tuning my grammar and tenses. Her Foreword is edifying and soul-winning.

To Georgette Ross and all Xlibris Staff who worked with me by urging me to persevere in my research and assured me that there are many people who will surely be nourished and inspired by the insight and ideas in my book. To Monsignor Gabriel Eche (1923-2004) whose life of humility inspires us still.

To all my friends and well wishers for your love and solidarity. May God shower His choicest blessings upon you and your families. So be it.

FOREWORD

"THE WAY TO Christ is first through humility, second through humility, third through humility. If humility does not precede and accompany and follow every good work we do, if it is not before us to focus on, if it is not beside us to lean upon, if it is not behind us to fence us in; pride will wrench from our hand any good deed we do at the very moment we do it". Saint Augustine (Letters 118:32).

Rev. Fr. Peter Obinna Umekwe has provided us with 240 inspirational quotations on humility. To receive faith one must be humble to know that he does not know everything. In a world that is now full of pride, arrogance, misuse of power—financial, political and cultural, humility has been pushed to the back seat.

The wars in the world—past and present, could be said to have been caused by lack of humility—the refusal to talk to and listen to others, to forgive and accommodate others. This book in a way advertises "the amazing strength in humility" and so, encourages people to be humble.

Pride is said to be the root of all evils, because from it all others grow. It turned Lucifer into Satan and banned him eternally from heaven. It was to replace this vice of pride that the Lord Jesus Christ came to us in humility . . . "though He was in the form of God, did not count equality with God, a thing to be grasped; but He emptied Himself, taking the form of a slave, becoming as human beings are".—Phil.2:6-7.

The quotations in this book cut across continents, the living and dead, cultures, races and religions. This shows that humility is tangibly universal, and not an exclusive reserve of particular persons or peoples.

In our daily contacts with people and in our international relations, we need humility to help us know who we are. In doing so, we would not lord it over others as the "pagans" do. I therefore, recommend this book to all and sundry, especially, young people and students.

—*Fr. Chukwudi O.Callistus Onwere.*
Pastor,St. Pius V Parish, Jacksonville, Florida.

My husband and I traveled to Rome in the spring of 2007 to have our marriage blessed by Pope Benedict. I was in the process of converting to Catholicism and wanted to celebrate my 30th wedding anniversary in Rome. Our Bishop had secured front row seats for us at the Wednesday Audience with Pope Benedict. As Catholic newlyweds, we were some of the first to shake the Pope's hand that day. Little did we know that we would meet someone else that day who would show us Christ's work in our lives.

Father Peter Obinna Umekwe stood behind us as we waited for the Pope to approach us. We met Father Peter for the first time that beautiful day in March, and we learned that he was just as excited to meet the Pope as we were. If one has not attended a Wednesday Audience with the Pope, he would not anticipate the crowding and pushing that accompanies such intense enthusiasm and anticipation.

We stood outside the Vatican with thousands of other people, hardly believing we were standing where so many others had come before us. When the ceremony ended, we got introduced with Fr.

Peter and eventually became friends. Furthermore, we, along with thousands of the faithful, went inside the Vatican to hear the Pope say Mass. Father Peter offered to assist us apply for and obtain the Papal Blessing Certificate. He promised to mail it to us as soon as he got it. After that, he took us inside the Vatican to pray with us.

Although we had been in the Vatican earlier on our trip, I felt complete awe when I looked toward the main altar and saw the Pope dressed in crimson robes. I heard the most beautiful music drifting toward us. Father Peter took us over to Michelangelo's Pieta and immediately fell to his knees. My husband and I each fell to our knees with Father kneeling between us. In addition to the glorious singing, I could hear my tears dropping onto the marble floor. With the Pope saying Mass to thousands of people in the background, Father Peter blessed our marriage. Yet, I felt like only three people were at what I now consider to be my wedding: my husband, myself, and Father Peter representing Christ.

Since that life-changing day in Rome, my husband and I have had the pleasure of entertaining Father Peter in our home and in our garden in Beaumont, Texas. Of all the places we offered to take him on his visit, he chose the Houston zoo. He used every minute of his visit to allow us to see Christ in him. I would assert that humility is Father Peter's most noticeable trait. His choices, his behavior, and his influence caused us to feel so comfortable in his presence. He showed us Christ's friendship and Christ's love. He truly loves serving others. His example stays in my thoughts and prayers every day. He is a blessing to our lives and hopefully will be to yours.

William Shakespeare wrote of humility in dozens upon dozens of lines in his plays. In classical times, Sophocles wrote of Oedipus's journey from arrogance to humility. In modern times, T. S. Eliot commented that "humility is the most difficult of all virtues to achieve." For thousands of years, we have pondered humility and its place in our lives. So it should be.

—Patricia Heintzelman.
Dept. of English and Modern Languages,
Lamar University Beaumont, Texas.

My friend, Father Peter Obinna Umekwe has compiled a wealth of inspirational quotes for us. Humility is a subject often neglected and this book reminds us of its importance. Our society preaches the significance of high self esteem and often overlooks the value of humility. These quotes remind us that through humility, we gain strength, purpose and fullness of spirit. Fr. Peter teaches us how to replace the pitfalls of pride with humility, gratitude and grace. This unique book inspires and challenges us to be true children of God.

—*Mary Beth Smith.*
Resource Conservationist, United States
Department of Agriculture Moro, Oregon.

Fr. Peter is a friend and brother. I live here in Condon where he serves and joyfully shares many of Gods gifts with folks in Gilliam and Wheeler Counties.

Fr. Obi, as I prefer to call him came from humble beginnings and is a humble man. Born in a small village in Nigeria where his mother still lives. He has worked tirelessly from a young age to become what he is today. He has devoted most of his adult life to learning the precepts and life in the seminary which led to his ordination as a Catholic Priest.

Like most of us, he loves his family and friends and sadly lost his father who was a prison officer (warder) in Nigeria. I have had the privilege and pleasure to meet and interact with some of his tribesmen who are also priests Including, Fr. Joseph and Fr. Charles and his, (Fr. Charles's) sister, Christine. It was a wonderful day!

Fr. Peter's passion for Christ, the scriptures and his desire to share the precious treasures contained in the Bible is inspiring. He has always been able to focus on a few passages that bring comfort and meaning to happenings in my life.

On some occasions, he has told me that I am a humble man. It is difficult to accept in the face of a man that has lifted me up, not being judgmental. When pressed about his humility, he only says, "I am still learning." He has touched many lives including mine. He has made me such a better man and for our friendship and brotherhood, I will always rejoice. His book on humility will be the first of many and I am so happy that he made it happen.

—*Loyd Smith.*
Ranch Manager,
Smith Family Farms Condon, Oregon.

INTRODUCTION

THE TERM HUMILITY, etymologically speaking, is derived from the Latin word, "humilitas", a noun related to the adjective "humilis", translated not only as "humble" but alternatively as "low" or "from the earth". Some authorities suggest that Catholic writings see humility connected to the cardinal virtue of temperance. Dictionary definitions of humility focus on a person's humble opinion of himself and his willingness to submit himself to God and to others for God's sake. Meekness and unpretentiousness serve as synonyms to humility while pride often serves as the antonym, or opposite, to humility.

Looking at what is going on in the world today, one finds it easy to observe that some societies put down humility and inordinately pursue "freedom". Nobody wants to obey anybody. People indiscriminately treat those in positions of authority with levity. Many children disobey their parents and resist their instructions and directions.

Some insubordinate children have gone to the extent of calling the police to arrest their parents. Often, people publicly and disrespectfully challenge and resist their superiors, bosses, and elders. We live in a world where people think more of themselves than others.

This situation where people either no longer show humility or find it difficult to embrace it is noticeable in families, schools, institutions, offices, organizations, relationships and, in fact, all facets of life. Nowadays, people find it difficult to humble themselves or to apologize even when it is obvious that they have done something wrong. Such people probably think that humility is a sign of weakness when, in truth, there is amazing strength in humility.

This amazing strength in humility provides the basis for what this book is poised to reveal to its readers. I wrote this book to encourage people to pursue this dying virtue. My mission is to remind my readers of the power of humility: the ideas are drawn from the Bible and from the powerful thoughts and wisdom of great scholars and various minds across time and space.

I pray God leads me down my own path to achieve humility. As most of us know, humility requires continuous and diligent effort. However, the rewards are worth the struggle. Among other things, humility removes pride from us and makes us worthy recipients of God's grace. I wish you a thrilling journey and ask that you remember the appeal of Jesus: *"learn from me, for I am gentle and humble in heart, and you will find rest for your souls"*—Matthew 11:29.

1

He that is humble, ever shall have God to be his guide.

—John Bunay.

2

The higher we are placed, the more humbly should we walk.

—Cicero.

3

Nearest the throne itself must be the footstool of humility.

—James Montgomery.

4

True humility is contentment.

—Henri Frederic Amiel.

5

Do you wish to rise? Begin by descending. You plan a tower that will piece the clouds? Lay first the foundation of humility.

—Saint Augustine.

6

There is something in humility which strangely exalts the heart.

—Saint Augustine.

7

Humility is the mark of a genuine disciple.

—Saint Thomas Aquinas.

8

The unassuming youth seeking instruction with humility gains good fortune.

—Joseph Addison.

9

There is no respect for others without humility in oneself.

—Henri Frederick Amiel.

10

Humility may bring you humiliation here on earth, but surely not in heaven.

—Bishop Michael Eneja.

11

Tell him on the contrary that he needs, in the interest of his own happiness, to walk in the path of humility and self-control.

—Irving Babbitt.

12

Humility is the solid foundation of all virtues.

—Kong Fuzi.

13

For in sacrifice, you take no delight, burnt offering from me, you would not desire; my sacrifice, a contrite spirit; a humbled contrite heart O lord, you will not spurn.

—Psalm 51:16-17.

14

The whole thing of this business is to retain your enthusiasm and, in a sense, retain your innocence and try to practice as much humility as possible.

—John Frankenheimer.

15

Pride perceiving humility honorable, often borrows her cloak.

—Thomas Fuller.

16

I claim to be a simple individual liable to err like any other fellow mortal. I own, however, that I have humility enough to confess my errors and to retrace my steps.

—Mohandas Gandhi.

17

We must admit with humility that, while number is purely a product of our minds, space has a reality outside of our minds, so that we cannot completely prescribe its properties a priori.

—Carl Friedrich Gauss.

18

Humility is really important because it keeps you fresh and new.

—Steven Tyler.

19

Judge yourself; if you sincerely and humbly do that, you will not be judged by God.

—Johannes Tauler.

20

In the school of the spirit, man learns wisdom through humility.

—Johannes Tauler.

21

We come nearest to the great, when we are great in humility.

—Rabindranath Togore.

22

When someone saves your life and gives you life, there is gratitude and humility; there is a time you've been so blessed you realize you've been given another chance in life that maybe, you did or did not deserve.

—Pat Summerall.

23

It takes humility and patience to listen to your little children talk to you with excitement about a matter of which you have no interest.

—Msgr. Gabriel Eche.

24

It is essential to employ, trust, and reward those whose perspectives, abilities and judgments are radically different from yours and perhaps, better than yours. It is also rare, for it requires uncommon humility, tolerance, and wisdom.

—Dee Hock.

25

If we learn not humility, we learn nothing.

—John Dewel.

26

Humility is a flower which does not grow in everyone's garden.

—Aristotle.

27

Humility is a priceless virtue; however, it takes a lot of self-emptying to cultivate it.

—Bishop Michael Eneja.

28

My soul proclaims the greatness of the Lord, and my spirit rejoices in God my Savior; because He has looked upon the lowliness of his servant; yes, from now onwards, all generations will call me blessed; for the Almighty has done great things for me; holy is His name.

—Luke 1:46-48.

29

Real genius is nothing else but the supernatural virtue of humility in the domain of thought.

—Simone Weil.

30

Humility is attentive patience.

—Simone Weil.

31

Humility is not thinking less of yourself; it is thinking of yourself less.

—Rick Warren.

32

One thing that golf teaches you is humility.

—Robert Warner.

33

One without humility is like a city broken into and left in ruins without walls.

—Unknown.

34

You probably have started losing touch with humility when your friends start avoiding you without telling you why.

—Archbishop Albert Obiefuna.

35

Do good by stealth, and blush to find it fame.

—Alexander Pope.

36

With courage you will dare to take risks, have the strength to be compassionate, and the wisdom to be humble. Courage is the foundation of integrity.

—Keshavan Nair.

37

It is unwise to be too sure of one's own wisdom. It is healthy to be reminded that the strongest might weaken and the wisest might err.

—Mohandas K. Gandhi.

38

It is a wholesome and necessary thing for us to turn again to the earth and in the contemplation of her beauties, to know of wonder and humility.

—Rachel Carson.

39

Religion is to do right. It is to love, it is to serve, it is to think, it is to be humble.

—Ralph Waldo Emerson.

40

The Lord favors the humble.

—Proverbs 3:34.

41

The higher a man is in grace, the lower he will be in his own esteem.

—Charles Haddon Spurgeon.

42

Humility is like a tree, whose root when it sets deepest in the earth rises higher, and spreads fairer and stands surer, and lasts longer, and every step of its descent is like a rib of iron.

—Jeremy Taylor.

43

A genuinely humble person humbles himself even before those who should be humbled by his presence.

—Bishop Michael Eneja.

44

Do you wish people to think well of you? Don't speak well of yourself.

—Blaise Pascal.

45

Humility is the gateway into the grace and favor of God.

—Harold Warner.

46

Humility before God is far more desirable than humiliation by our sin.

—Ron Clark.

47

Humility is the ladder to divine understanding.

—Unknown.

48

If you are right, take the humble side—you will help the other fellow; if you are wrong, take the humble side—and you will help yourself.

—Unknown.

49

When we become aware of our humility, we've lost it.

—Unknown.

50

We come nearest to the greatest when we are great in humility.

—Rabindranath Tagore.

51

When the news of Jonah's preaching reached the king of Nineveh, he rose from his throne, took off his robe, put on sack-clothe and sat down in ashes.

—Jonah 3:6.

52

Remain humble, even when you are persecuted because of your humility.

—Bishop Michael Eneja.

53

"You are unrepentantly stubborn, intransigent and incorrigible". Humble people correct their mistakes early enough that they don't give others opportunity to talk to them this way.

—Bruce Anderson.

54

Those who irrevocably cling to their ego lose God's grace and deny themselves the help, support, and favor they would have gotten if they had showed humility.

—Nancy Campbell.

55

People may sometimes laugh at you, make caricature of you and put you down because you showed humility, but did you do the right thing, of course, yes.

—Virginia Jordan.

56

Those who resist humility and embrace stubbornness are slaves. Their liberation is in their own hands.

—Nicholas Lamb.

57

The principles of living greatly include the capacity to face trouble with courage, disappointment with cheerfulness, and trial with humility.

—Unknown.

58

Humility is the altar upon which God wishes that we offer Him His sacrifice.

—Francois duc de la Rochefoucauld.

59

Humility is the root, mother, nurse, foundation, and bond of all virtues.

—Saint John Chrysostom.

60

What makes humility so desirable is the marvelous thing it does for us; it creates in us a capacity for the closest possible intimacy with God.

—Monica Baldwin.

61

True humility is intelligent self respect which keeps us from thinking too highly or too meanly of ourselves. It makes us modest by reminding us how far we have come short of what we can be.

—Ralph W. Sockman.

62

The churches must learn humility as well as teach it.

—George Bernard Shaw.

63

Humility must be the portion of any man who receives acclaim earned in the blood of his followers and the sacrifices of his friends.

—Dwight David Eisenhower.

64

Do not destroy him; for who can stretch out his hand against the Lord's anointed, and be guiltless.

—1 Samuel 26:9.

65

Humility leads to strength and not to weakness. It is the highest form of self-respect to admit mistakes and to make amends for them.

—John J. McCloy.

66

Humility is the only true wisdom by which we prepare our minds for all the possible changes of life.

—George Arliss.

67

There is no gardening without humility. Nature is constantly sending even its oldest scholars to the bottom of the class for some egregious blunder.

—Alfred Austin.

68

My power will be in humility.

—Walter Russell.

69

In a humble state, you learn better.

—John Dooner.

70

The grace that makes every grace amiable is humility.

—John Ruskin.

71

I believe the first test of a truly great man is humility.

—John Ruskin.

72

In humility, imitate Jesus and Socrates.

—Benjamin Franklin.

73

Humility and resignation are our prime virtues.

—John Dryden.

74

He that places himself neither higher nor lower than he ought to do exercises truest humility.

—Charles Caleb Cotton.

75

True humility—the basis of the Christian system—is the low but deep and firm foundation of all virtues.

—Edmund Burke.

76

Who am I and what is my lineage—and my father's family in Israel—for me to become the king's son-in-law?

—1 Samuel 18:18.

77

Humility is to make a right estimate of one's self.

—Charles Hadden Spurgeon.

78

Humility, that low, sweet root, from which all heavenly virtues shoot.

—Thomas More.

79

Wash out your ego every once in a while, as cleanliness to godliness not just in body but in humility as well.

—Abbe Yeux-Verdi.

80

Humility makes great men twice honorable.

—Benjamin Franklin.

81

Humility is the solid foundation of all the virtues.

—Confucius.

82

Humility leads to the highest distinction, because it leads to self-improvement.

—Sir Benjamin Collins Brodie.

83

Even if you be otherwise perfect, you fail without humility.

—The Talmud.

84

Life is a long lesson in humility.

—James m. Barrie.

85

It is good for me Lord, that thou hast humbled me, that I may learn thy righteous judgments, and may cast away all haughtiness of heart and all presumption.

—Thomas A'Kempis.

86

Humility is the secret of fellowship, and pride the secret of division.

—Robert C. Chapman.

87

Obedience is the road to freedom, humility the road to pleasure, unity the road to personality.

—C.S. Lewis.

88

The meek man is not a human mouse afflicted with a sense of his own inferiority. Rather he may be in his moral life as bold as a lion and as strong as Sampson; but he has stopped being fooled about himself. He has accepted God's estimate of his own life.

—A. W. Tozer.

89

Be desirous, my son, to do the will of another rather than thy own.

—Thomas A'Kempis.

90

How great victory was that which Jonathan must have gained over himself, when he rejoiced to see David raised above him! He discerned the mind of God in David, and had so learned to delight in God, that he did not see in David one who was to outshine him, but another faithful man raised up for God and Israel.

—Robert C. Chapman.

91

God created the world out of nothing, and so long as we are nothing, He can make something out of us.

—Martin Luther.

92

After all, man knows very little, and may some day learn enough of his own ignorance to fall down and pray.

—Henry Adams.

93

The sufficiency of my merit is to know that my merit is not sufficient.

—Saint Augustine.

94

Revival is a renewed conviction of sin and repentance, followed by an intense desire to live in obedience to God. It is giving up one's will to God in deep humility.

—Charles Finney.

95

Should you ask me what is the first thing in religion, I should reply that the first, second, and third thing therein is humility.

—Saint Augustine.

96

People who regard themselves as invalids rather than heroes will make excellent missionaries.

—Daniel Fuller.

97

A man can counterfeit love, he can counterfeit faith, he can counterfeit hope and all the other graces, but it is very difficult to counterfeit humility.

—D.L. Moody.

98

We ought not be weary in doing little things for the love of God, who regards not the greatness of the work, but the love with which it is performed.

—Brother Lawrence.

99

How do we know if we have a servant's heart? By how we act when we are treated like one.

—Father John Corapi.

100

The only humility that is really ours is not that which we try to show before God in prayer, but that which we carry with us in our daily conduct.

—Andrew Murray.

101

Be not proud of race, face, place, or grace.

—Charles Haddon Spurgeon.

102

Be not angry that you cannot make others as you wish them to be, since you cannot always make yourself as you wish to be.

—Thomas A. Kempis.

103

The meek man will attain a place of soul rest. As he walks on in meekness, he will be happy to let God defend him. The old struggle to defend himself is over. He has found the peace which meekness brings.

—A. W. Tozer.

104

How tragic that the very thing that could set us free—playing the fool—is the thing we will not do. When we are afraid to be fools, we end up being afraid to be anything.

—Mike Mason.

105

I am sure that there are many Christians who will confess that their experiences have been very much like my own—that we had long known the Lord without realizing that meekness and lowliness of heart should be the distinguishing features of the disciple, as they were of the Master. Such humility is not a thing that will come on its own. It must be made the object of special desire, prayer, faith, and practice.

—Andrew Murray.

106

God descends to the humble as waters flow down from the hills into the valleys.

—Tikhon.

107

We have forgotten the gracious hand which has preserved us in peace and multiplied and enriched and strengthened us, and have vainly imagined in the deceitfulness of our hearts that all these blessings were produced by some superior wisdom and virtue of our own. Intoxicated with unbroken success, we have become too self sufficient to feel the necessity of redeeming and preserving Grace, too proud to pray to the God that made us.

—Abraham Lincoln.

108

The proof of spiritual maturity is not how pure you are but awareness of your impurity. That very awareness opens the door to grace.

—Philip Yancey.

109

Humility is freedom from your own driven ego.

—Martha Kilpatrick.

110

Humility is nothing else but a right judgment of ourselves.

—William Law.

111

Humility is offering no resistance to the dealings of the Lord with us.

—William Law.

112

Those who have known God without knowing their wretchedness have not glorified Him, but have glorified themselves.

—Blaise Pascal.

113

The devil sees nothing more abominable than a truly humble Christian, for that Christian is just the opposite of the devil's own image.

—Hans Nielsen Hauge.

114

There is no room for God in him who is full of himself.

—Martin Buber.

115

God is not proud. He will have us even though we have shown we prefer everything else to Him.

—C. S. Lewis.

116

We are to be as unnoticed as the Lord was at times. We should be willing to pass through the crowd and not be noticed.

—W.A. Belle.

117

Provided God is glorified, we must not care by whom.

—Francis de Sales.

118

We must make humility the chief thing we admire in Jesus.

—Andrew Murray.

119

A humble knowledge of ourselves is a surer way to God than is the search for depth of learning.

—Thomas A'Kempis.

120

Without humility of heart, all the other virtues by which one runs toward God seem—and are—absolutely worthless.

—Angelo of Foligno.

121

Whoever exalts himself will be humbled; but whoever humbles himself will be exalted.

—Matthew 23:12.

122

At a glance, bring down all the proud. Strike down the wicked where they stand.

—Job 40:12.

123

But the meek will inherit the land and enjoy great peace.

—Psalm 37:11.

124

Just like the saying goes that those who want to be great should be ready to pay the price, I would say that those who do not want to be humble should also be ready to pay the price.

—Lawrence Smith.

125

You rebuke the arrogant, who are cursed and who stray from your commands.

—Psalm 119:21.

126

My heart is not proud, O Lord, nor haughty my eyes, I have not gone after things too great, nor marvels beyond me.

—Psalm 131:1.

127

Though the Lord is on high, He looks upon the lowly, but the proud, He knows from afar.

—Psalm 138:6.

128

The Lord sustains the humble but casts the wicked to the ground.

—Psalm 147:6.

129

For the Lord takes delight in His people; He crowns the humble with salvation.

—Psalm 149:4.

130

Humility is admired by everyone including the proud. Have you observed that even employers who are so full of themselves admire their humble employees the most. What a world!

—Thomas Jordan.

131

To fear the Lord is to hate evil; I hate evil and arrogance, evil behavior and perverse speech.

—Proverbs 8:13.

132

When pride comes, then comes disgrace, but with humility comes wisdom.

—Proverbs 11:2.

133

Humility comes before honor.

—Proverbs 15:33.

134

Pride goes before destruction; a haughty spirit before a fall.

—Proverbs 16:18.

135

Before his downfall, a man's heart is proud; but humility comes before honor.

—Proverbs 18:12.

136

Humility and the fear of the Lord bring wealth and honor and life.

—Proverbs 22:4.

137

He guides the humble in what is right and teaches them His way.

—Proverbs 25:9.

138

Let another praise you, not your own mouth; someone else,

and not your own lips.

—Proverbs 27:2.

139

Pride ends in a fall, while humility brings honor.

—Proverbs 29:23.

140

"Has not my hands made all these things, and so they came into being?" declares the Lord. "This is the one I esteem: he who is humble and contrite in spirit, and trembles at my word."

—Isaiah 66:2.

141

He has showed you, O man, what is good. And what does the Lord require of you? To act justly and to love mercy and to work humbly with your God.

—Micah 6:8.

142

And he said, "I tell you the truth, unless you change and become like little children, you will never enter the kingdom of heaven. Therefore whoever humbles himself like this little child is the greatest in the kingdom of heaven."

—Matthew 18:3-4.

143

He has brought down rulers from their thrones but has lifted up the humble.

—Luke 1:52.

144

When He noticed how the guests picked the places of honor at the table, He told them this parable: "When someone invites you to a wedding feast, do not take the place of honor, for a person more distinguished than you may have been invited. If so, the host who invited both of you will come and say to you, 'Give this man your seat.' Then humiliated, you will have to take the least important place. But when you are invited, take the lowest place. So that when the host comes, he will say to you, 'Friend, move up to a better place.' Then you will be honored in the presence of all your fellow guests. For everyone who exalts himself will be humbled, and he who humbles himself, will be exalted."

—Luke 14:7-11.

145

He said to them, "You are the ones who justify yourselves in the eyes of men, but God knows your hearts. What is highly valued among men is detestable in God's sight.

—Luke 16:15.

146

To some who were confident of their own righteousness and looked down on everyone else Jesus told this parable, "Two men went up to the temple to pray, one, a Pharisee and the other, a tax collector. The Pharisee stood up and prayed thus: 'God, I thank you that I am not like the other men—robbers, evil doers, adulterers—or even like this tax collector. I fast twice a week and give one tenth of all I get.'" But the tax collector stood at a distance. He would not even look up to heaven, but beat his breast and said, "God, have mercy on me, a sinner. "I tell you that this man rather than the other, went home justified before God. For everyone who exalts himself will be humbled, and he who humbles himself will be exalted.

—Luke 18:9-14.

147

Also a dispute arose among them as to which of them was considered to be the greatest. Jesus said to them, "Among the gentiles, it is the kings who lord it over them, and those who have authority over them are given the title, benefactor. With you, this must not happen. No: the greatest among you must behave as if he were the youngest, the leader as if he were the one who serves. For who is the greater: the one at table or the one who serves? The one at table, surely? Yet here am I among you as one who serves!"

—Luke 22:24-27.

148

Sitting down, Jesus called the Twelve and said, "If anyone wants to be first, he must be the very last, and the servant of all.

—Mark 9:35.

149

For by the grace given to me, I say to every one of you: Do not think of yourself more highly than you ought, but rather think of yourself with sober judgment, in accordance with the measure of faith God has given you.

—Romans 12:3.

150

Live in harmony with one another. Do not be proud, but be willing to associate with people of low position.

—Romans 12:16.

151

He chose the lowly things of this world and the despised things—and the things that are not—to nullify the things that are.

—1 Corinthians 1:28.

152

Love is patient, love is kind. It does not envy, it does not boast, it is not proud.

—1 Corinthians 13:4.

153

I am content in weaknesses, insults, hardships, persecutions and difficulties for Christ's sake. For when I am weak, then I am strong.

—2 Corinthians 12:10.

154

Since we live by the spirit, let us keep in step with the spirit. Let us not become conceited, provoking and envying one another.

—Galatians 5:25-26.

155

May I never boast except in the cross of our Lord Jesus Christ, through which the world has been crucified to me, and I to the world.

—Galatians 6:14.

156

Be completely humble and gentle; be patient, bearing with one another in love.

—Ephesians 4:2.

157

If you have any encouragement from being united with Christ, if any comfort from his love, if any fellowship with spirit, if any tenderness and compassion, then make joy complete by being like-minded, having the same love, being one in spirit and purpose. Do nothing out of selfish ambition or vain conceit, but in humility, consider others better than yourselves.

—Philippians 2:1-3.

158

The attitude that you should have is the one that Christ Jesus had: "Though he was in the form of God, he did not count equality with God, something to be grasped. But he emptied himself, taking the form of a servant, becoming as human beings are. He humbled himself and became obedient unto death, even death on a cross. Therefore, God highly exalted him, and gave him the name which is above all other names.

—Philippians 2:5-9.

159

Therefore, as God's chosen people, holy and dearly loved, clothe yourselves with compassion, kindness, humility, gentleness, and patience.

—Colossians 3:12.

160

But he gives us more grace. That is why the Scriptures say: "God opposes the proud but gives grace to the humble."

—James 4:6.

161

I urge the elders among you, as a fellow-elder myself and a witness to the sufferings of Christ, and as one who is to have a share in the glory that is to be revealed: Give a shepherd's care to the flock of God that is entrusted to you; watch over it, not simply as a duty but gladly, as God wants; not for sordid money, but because you are eager to do it. Do not lord it over to the group which is in your charge, but be an example for the flock. When the chief shepherd appears, you will be given the unfading crown of glory.

—1 Peter 5:1-4.

162

In the same way, younger people, be submissive to the elders. All of you, clothe yourselves with humility toward one another, because, "God opposes the proud but gives grace to the humble." Humble yourselves therefore, under God's mighty hand, that He may lift you up in due time.

—1 Peter 5:5-6.

163

Blessed are the meek, for they shall inherit the earth.

Matthew 5:5.

164

Let he that standeth take heed, lest he falls.

—I Corinthians 10:12.

165

It must be felt that there is no national security but in the nation's humble acknowledged dependence upon God and His overruling providence.

—John Adams.

166

It takes humility to seek feedback. It takes wisdom to understand it, analyze it, and appropriately act on it.

—Stephen R. Covey.

167

The road to success leads through the valley of humility, and the path is up the ladder of patience and across the wide barren plains of perseverance. As yet, no short cut has been discovered.

—Joseph J. Lamb.

168

Affliction is the wholesome soil of virtue, where patience, honor, sweet humility, and calm attitude take root and strongly flourish.

—David Mallet.

169

Assuredly, loving souls, you should go to God with all humility and respect, humbling yourself in his presence, especially, when you remember your past ingratitude and sins.

—Alphonsus Liguori.

170

I think we all need to be a part of the suffering and the solution. We need more humility as Americans.

—Billy Jackson.

171

I beg the Most High to allow me the favor of the double reward, but if God only finds me worthy of one reward, I will accept it in all humility.

—King Hassan 11.

172

There are no better cosmetics than a severe temperance and purity, modesty and humility, a generous temper and calmness of spirit; and there is no true beauty without the signatures of these graces in the very countenance.

—Arthur Helps.

173

It was pride that changed angels into devils. It is humility that makes men angels.

—Saint Augustine.

174

Humility is the foundation of all other virtues; hence, in the soul in which this virtue does not exist, there cannot be any other virtue except in mere appearance.

—Saint Augustine.

175

My favored temple is a humble heart.

—Philip James Bailey.

176

Lowliness is the base of every virtue; and he who goes the lowest builds the safest.

—Philip James Bailey.

177

By humility and the fear of the Lord, are riches and honor and life.

—Proverbs 22:4.

178

Humility leads to the highest distinction, because it leads to self-improvement.

—Sir Benjamin Collins Brodie.

179

"He that humbleth himself shall be exalted." This great law of the kingdom of God is, in the teaching of Christ, inscribed over its entrance-gate.

—Sir Thomas Browne.

180

True humility—the basis of the Christian system—is the low but deep and firm foundation of all virtues.

—Edmund Burke.

181

True love is the parent of a noble humility.

—William Ellery Channing.

182

The street is full of humiliation to the proud.

—Ralph Waldo Emerson.

183

It is in vain to gather virtues without humility; for the spirit of God delighteth to dwell in the hearts of the humble.

—Desiderius Gerhard Erasmus.

184

To be humble to our superiors, is duty; to our equals, courtesy; to our inferiors, generosity.

—Owen Felltham (Feltham.

185

The most essential point is lowliness.

—Francois de Salignac Fenelon.

186

They that know God will be humble; they that know themselves cannot be proud.

—Rev. John Flavel (2).

187

After crosses and losses, men grow humbler and wiser.

—Benjamin Franklin.

188

God has sworn to lift on high, who sinks himself by true humility.

—John Keble.

189

Whatever obscurities may involve religious tenets, humility and love constitute the essence of true religion; the humble is formed to adore, the loving to associate with eternal love.

—Johann Kaspar Lavater (John Caspar Lavater).

190

God's sweet dews and showers of grace slide off the mountain of pride, and fall on the low valleys of the humble hearts, and make them pleasant and fertile.

—Archbishop Robert Leighton.

191

If thou wouldst find much favor and peace with God and man, be very low in thine own eyes; forgive thyself little, and others much.

—Archbishop Robert Leighton.

192

Humility is always grace, always dignity.

—James Russell Lowell.

193

O be very sure that no man will learn anything at all, unless he first will learn humility.

—Lord Edward Robert Bulwer Lytton.

194

Pride makes us artificial and humility makes us real.

—Thomas Merton.

195

An able and yet humble man is a jewel worth a kingdom.

—William Penn.

196

There is nothing so clear-sighted and sensible as a noble mind in a low estate.

—Jane Porter.

197

The high mountains are barren, but the low valleys are covered over with corn; and accordingly, the showers of God's grace fall into lowly hearts and humble souls.

—Worthington.

198

Humility leads to strength and not to weakness. It is the highest form of self-respect to admit mistakes and to make amends for them.

—John J. McCloy.

199

A man who is at the top is a man who has the habit of getting to the bottom.

—Joseph E. Rogers.

200

If thou desireth the love of God and man, be humble. The voice of humility is God's music, and the silence of humility is God's rhetoric.

—Francis Quarles.

201

A humble person is totally different from a person who cannot recognize and appreciate himself as part of this world's marvels.

—Rabino Nilton Bonder.

202

Pride is concerned with *who is right*. Humility is concerned with *what is right*.

—Ezra Taft Benson.

203

Humility is royalty without a crown.

—Spencer W. Kimball.

204

Humility is: Greatness in plain clothes.

—Spencer W. Kimball.

205

Fullness of knowledge always and necessarily means some understanding of the depths of our ignorance, and that is always conducive to both humility and reverence.

—Robert A. Millikan.

206

He who sacrifices a whole-offering, shall be rewarded for a whole-offering; he who offers a burnt-offering shall have the reward of a burnt offering; but he who offers humility to God and man shall be rewarded with a reward as if he had offered all the sacrifices in the world.

—The Talmud.

207

Some persons are always ready to level those above them down to themselves, while they are never willing to level those below them up to their own position. But he that is under the influence of true humility will avoid both of these extremes. On the one hand, he will be willing that all should rise just so far as their diligence and worth of character entitle them to; and on the other hand, he will be willing that his superiors should be known and acknowledged in their place, and have rendered to them all the honors that are their due.

—Jonathan Edwards.

208

People are easily impressed by the way someone looks, but real leadership comes from what is inside a person—from the heart. Consider the shepherd who became king David.

—Ken Treybig.

209

"You come to me with sword, spear, and scimitar, but I come to you in the name of Yahweh Sabaoth, God of the armies of Israel, whom you have challenged."

—1 Samuel 17: 45.

210

Through failure, we learn a lesson in humility which is probably needed, painful though it is.

—Bill Wilson.

211

It is very difficult for the prosperous to be humble.

—Jane Austen.

212

Humility and knowledge in poor clothes excel pride and ignorance in costly attire.

—William Penn.

213

Humility is not cowardice. Meekness is not weakness. Humility and meekness are indeed spiritual powers.

—Swami Sivananda.

214

Humility is the ability and the willingness to learn.

—Charlie Sheen.

215

Religion in its humility restores man to his only dignity, the courage to live by grace.

—George Santayana.

216

Too many people in government seem to think that they are above regular folks, and I said I would expect humility in the way each member of the team served—that they would recognize that the tax payer is the boss.

—Mark Sanford.

217

The best loved by God are those that are rich, yet have the humility of the poor, and those that are poor and have the magnanimity of the rich.

—Saadi.

218

To be a preacher requires two apparently contradictory qualities: confidence and humility.

—Timothy Radcliffe.

219

It becomes us in humility to make our devout acknowledgements to the Supreme Ruler of the Universe for the inestimable civil and religious blessings with which we are favored.

—James Polk.

220

Philanthropic humility is necessary if a giver is to do more good than harm, but it is not sufficient—philanthropic prudence is also needed.

—Marvin Olasky.

221

Humility is one of the virtues most admired and held up as an example among Jews since biblical times. Moses is described as "a very humble man more so than any other men on earth" (Numbers 12:3); and precisely for this reason, the rabbis said, he was deemed worthy of receiving the Torah. Jeremiah likewise revealed this inner quality when he proved hesitant of undertaking his Divine Mission. The Talmudic sages regarded humility as an essential attribute of a scholar. Meekness provides a key to the afterlife (Sanh. 88b) and this virtue is attributed to God Himself." Wherever you find in Scripture of the power of God mentioned, there too you will find a reference to His humility."

—Mekhilta de-Rabbi Shimon bar Yohai; cf. Shab. 67a.

222

In Buddhism, humility is equivalent to a concern of how to be liberated from the sufferings of life and the vexation of the human mind. The ultimate aim is to achieve a state of enlightenment through meditation and other spiritual practices. When one experiences the ultimate Emptiness and non-self, one is free from suffering, vexation and all illusions of self-deception. Humility, compassion and wisdom characterize this state of enlightenment. "Enlightenment can come only after humility—the wisdom of realizing one's own ignorance, insignificance and lowliness, without which one cannot see the truth."

—Chan (Zen) Master Li Yuansong.

223

In peace, there's nothing so becomes a man as modest stillness and humility.

—William Shakespeare.

224

Humility is the virtue by which a man knowing himself as he truly is, abases himself. Jesus Christ is the ultimate definition of humility.

—Saint Berbard.

225

The virtue of humility consists in keeping oneself within one's own bounds, not reaching out to things above one, but submitting to one's superior.

—Saint Thomas Aquinas.

226

Legitimate humility comprises the following behaviors and attitudes: Submission to God and legitimate authorities; recognition of the virtues and talents that others possess, particularly those which surpass one's own, and giving due honor and, when required, obeisance; recognition of the limits of one's talents, ability or authority; and not reaching for that which is beyond one's grasp.

—Joseph Rickaby.

227

Successful indeed are the believers; those who humble themselves in their prayers.

—Qur'an, Al-Muminoon 23:1-2.

228

"According to Sikhism, all have to bow in humility before God. The fruit of humility is intuitive peace and pleasure. With humility they continue to meditate on the Lord, the Treasure of excellence. The God-conscious being is steeped in humility."

—Guru Nanak.

229

Rebellion, most of the time is borne out of lack of humility.

—Unknown.

230

Humility is the one companion without who most people have crash-landed in life.

—Unknown.

231

Life has its unpredictable way of exposing us to humility. Some people intentionally embrace it, some others are brought to it by circumstances.

—Unknown.

232

Humility helps us to serve a cause that is greater than our self-interest.

—Senator John McCain.

233

We all have our weak-points. Humility nevertheless, is the one virtue without which nobody may really experience true peace of mind.

—Unknown.

234

One bereft of humility will always find obedience difficult.

—Unknown.

235

Humility is a virtue, and indeed, a central virtue.

—Emmanuel Kant.

236

"Humility is considered an important virtue in Taoism. A wise person acts without claiming the result as his; he achieves his merit and does not rest arrogantly in it—he does not wish to display his superiority."

—Tao Te Ching.

237

It is easier to apologize to your superior than your subordinate. Those who express their apologies to both the former and the latter have truly known humility.

—Unknown.

238

John Vianney's humble beginning was indeed humble.

—Bishop Thomas J. Olmsted of Phoenix.

239

Fairest and best adorned is she whose clothing is humility.

—James Montgomery.

240

Those whose palm kernels were cracked by benevolent spirits should not forget to be humble.

—Chinua Achebe.

CONCLUSION

I N MY LIFE experiences, in my travels and while I was researching for this book, I have discovered that God is deeply drawn to the humble. He clearly states in several places in the Scriptures that He resists the proud and favors the humble. Humility is a virtue everybody should aspire to acquire. Even as I personally struggle with pride, I believe the ideas in this book will help me in my pursuit of humility. It is obvious that God uses the humble in powerful ways that surpass our human understanding and rationality.

This "virtue of virtues" should be our inseparable companion. Had *humility* been applied, so many divorces would have been avoided; so many broken relationships would have been healed; so many conflicts would have been resolved; so many people who were fired from their jobs or expelled from their positions, schools, organizations, or institutions would have been forgiven; so many privileges, opportunities, and favors denied folks in the past would have been secured; so many health issues like heart-attacks, high blood pressure, nervousness etc, would have been remedied and so many regrettable things that have happened in our lives and in our society would have been avoided.

My dear readers, "this is our chance." Humility is golden and it pays. We all need to be humble, old and young, parents and children, employers and employees, superiors and subordinates, guardians and wards, religious and state leaders, great and small. Let us embrace the virtue of humility. I wish I will always acknowledge my faults in humility and take pro-active actions to get over them!

Humility will help us, it will heal us, it will save us, and it will bring peace into our homes, families, offices, relationships, and world. Do not just read about humility; humbly pray to God in the silence of your heart to use the ideas here-in to positively transform your life; believe it will happen and it surely will happen.

One of the things this book will do for you is that it will help you to realize the value and power of humility. It will also help *you realize that humility is not a mark of weakness*. It will open your eyes to the amazing strength in humility. It will help you to cultivate the *"Be quick to apologize attitude"*. This new attitude of being quick to apologize to those you have offended or those you have hurt their feelings requires humility and it will help you to create a better relationship with them. It will surely take you to a whole new level of tranquility with God and folks.

If you know you offended somebody and you adamantly refuse to apologize, what do we call it? … of course, it is lack of humility… and when that happens, resentment will start building up in the mind of the offended which could have been avoided if you had humbled yourself and apologized. People are fairly easy to deal with… once you apply humility in your interactions/relationships with people, you will enjoy uncommon/priceless peace of mind.

To get in touch with your true self and enjoy profound peace of mind, you must have to kill the ego in you. Ego and humility cannot be room-mates. Where one is fostered, the other is defeated. Experience is the best teacher. If you keep an open mind and humbly apply the ideas in this book to your life situations and relationships, you will surely be the better and happier for it.

The therapist you need right now is you. Please keep this book handy so that you can re-read it from time to time. Give it to someone you love as a gift. Remember, we all have every reason to be humble because *we all had our humble beginnings.* May God bless you.

AUTHOR'S BIOGRAPHY

EARLY LIFE

FATHER PETER OBINNA Umekwe was born to Chief Nicholas Onyemachi Umekwe (of blessed memory) and Mrs Elizabeth Janet Umekwe on May 25, 1968 at Umuode Nsulu, Isiala Ngwa North Local Government Area of Abia State, Nigeria. He is the third male child and the fifth of seven children.

His birth took place during the Nigerian Civil War or the Nigerian-Biafran War, which lasted from July 6, 1967 until January 15, 1970. He was brought up in a traditional Catholic family. His early life was a mixed-bag of experiences. He lived partly with his parents, then with his paternal grand-mother, Maria Uchegbuo who actually raised him. He did his primary education at Community School Umuode Nsulu and his high school at Umunna Comprehensive Secondary School, Umuosu Nsulu.

While he was living with his grand-mother, his uncle's wife, Rachael Onwuegbuchi (who, owing to some surgery-complications at her first pregnancy lost her baby and could not have any more babies) came with her husband, Dee Levi to request his grand-mother to allow him live with them and his grand-mother, in her compassion yielded.

While he lived with his uncle and his wife, they treated him tenderly as their child since they did not at that time have a child of their own. He lived with them for some years and in his early teens returned to his grand-mother with whom he lived until he completed High School in 1985 (aged 17)and then joined his dad in Lagos in search of greener pastures.

INTERACTION WITH HIS GRAND-FATHER

While he lived with his grand-mother, he took care of his grand-father, Matthew Umekwe Uchegbuo who, at that time accidentally fell down from a raffia tree and became home-bound as a result of that.

He shaved the beards of his grand-father, barbed his hair, cut his nails, bathed him, fed him, washed his clothes and listened to his numerous stories blended with wise sayings. His closeness to his grand-father offered him the privilege of learning and knowing many of those Igbo aphorisms and wise sayings.

HIS GRAND-FATHER'S SPECIAL BLESSING

Above all, his grand-father gave him special blessing during his services to him. One day, he came into his grand-father's room to attend to him, his grand-father asked him to kneel down, he complied and the old man asked him to open his two palms, he obeyed and the old man prayed for him and spat into his palms and asked him to rob it on his (Obinna's)face. He was so dumbfounded at the unexpected gesture. All he could manage to say was, Amen! To this day, that incident not only edifies him but gives him chills whenever he remembers it.

LIFE AFTER SECONDARY SCHOOL (HIGH SCHOOL)

His father being a prison officer lives in the barracks wherever he is posted together with other officers. His mother lives partly with his father wherever he is and partly in the village to farm.

Coming from a large family, he did not always have enough to eat and drink with his brothers and sisters. Though his father was a Senior Inspector of Prisons (SIP), at Maximum/Medium Security Prisons Service Kirikiri Apapa, Lagos State, his salary was not sufficient to meet up with all the financial demands of his family. Therefore, his father whenever he was off from his regular job, kept his officers uniform aside and humbly engaged in all kinds of manual labour for money with his children in order to put food on the table.

As it were, Obinna was profoundly influenced by his father's dogged determination to survive despite the trying times he and his wife had raising their seven children. So Obinna and his brothers and sisters followed their father's good example of undying hard work in order to survive. He (Obinna) combined so many things to keep his head above sea-level at that time.

Having cleared his "Ordinary Level" papers the same year that he graduated from High School, he worked as a private lesson teacher in two families. He taught the children of Rev. Francis Okeremgbu (Pastor of Assemblies of God Church, kirikiri Apapa Lagos) 4:00pm-5:30pm and went over to the family of Chief and Lolo Nnabuife who lived some blocks away from the pastors house to teach their children from 6:00pm-7:30pm, Tuesday through Friday.

On Mondays and Saturdays, 4:00 pm-5:00pm, he worked as a substitute teacher in an Extra-Moral Class private school. There, he taught Economics and Christian Religious Knowledge to students preparing for GCE (General Certificate of Education) examination.

Other things he did before entering the seminary include, being a sales boy to his older cousin, Obisike Nwogbe who deals then in foreign T-Shirts near Mandilas in Lagos Mainland; cutting and distributing Palm-fronds in Lagos swamps for money to people who needed it. While he did all that, he did not forget his goal of advancing his education.

He sat for and passed JAMB (Joint Admission and Matriculation Board) examination in 1989 and was given admission to pursue a bachelors degree in English-Education in Alvan Ikoku College of Education Owerri under the auspices of University of Nigeria Nsukka. It was this course he was doing before God brought Rev. Fr. Callistus Nwachukwu (on Apostolic Work then in his village as a senior seminarian) his way, who helped in the discernment of his vocation to the priesthood at the age of twenty two.

ADMISSION INTO THE SEMINARY CUM SEMINARY FORMATION

He was interviewed and admitted into the seminary by Monsignor Ralph Nwosu, who was the Rector of Annunciation Seminary Amaudara then, July 1990. His seminary formation took him eleven years before he was ordained a priest, (1 year Prefecting, 1990, Annunciation Seminary Amaudara, 1 year, Spiritual Year, 1991, Nativity Spiritual Year Seminary Ozuabam, 4 years of philosophical studies, 1992/1996, Bigard Memorial Seminary Enugu, 1 year, Diocesan Assignment, 1996/1997, Annunciation Seminary Amaudara and 4 years of theological studies, 1997/2001, Bigard Memorial Seminary Enugu.

While a student of Bigard, he belonged to Don Scotus School of Journalism. Through this school, he advanced his studies in Journalism/Mass Communication; and before he completed his formation in Bigard, he also bagged a Higher National Diploma, HND in Mass Communication from Enugu State School of Journalism under the auspices of Enugu State University of Science and Technology, ESUTH.

He also has Masters degree in Pastoral Communication, Catholic Institute of West Africa, CIWA, Port Harcourt, 2003/2005 and Certificate in Italian Language from Pontifical Urban University, Rome, 2006.

PRIESTLY ORDINATION

Having successfully completed his seminary formation in June 2001, he was ordained a priest in the order of Melchisedech on Saturday, July 14, 2001 for the Catholic Diocese of Aba, Nigeria by Most Reverend Vincent V.Ezeonyia, CSSP, Catholic Bishop of Aba at Christ the King Cathedral Aba.

PASTORAL ASSIGNMENTS

Thirteen days after his priestly ordination, his Bishop, Most Reverend Vincent V. Ezeonyia assigned him to be one of the Parochial Vicars at Christ the King Cathedral Aba, 2001/2006; Chaplain, Catholic Media Workers, Catholic Diocese of Aba, 2002/2006; Chaplain, CKC Block Rosary Society, 2005/2006; Co-Vocations Director, Catholic Diocese of Aba, 2006; and presently, Administrator, St. John Parish Condon Oregon since 2007.

JOURNALISM CAREER

Having been assigned to Annunciation Seminary Amaudara by his Bishop after his philosophical studies as an auxiliary teacher, he shared with the students his passion for journalism and public speaking by founding a Press Club. This gave the students who joined the Club opportunities to express themselves by writing articles, engaging in debates and concerts under his supervision, 2006/2007; He was Staff Reporter, Don Scotus School of Journalism, Bigard, 1998/2000; Deputy Editor, Thinker Magazine, Bigard, 1994/1995; Deputy editor, Torch Magazine, Bigard, 1999/2000; Editor-in-Chief, Torch Magazine, Bigard, 2000—early 2001; Editorial Adviser from the time he handed over till June 2001 at his graduation; Editor-in-Chief, Rex Newspaper, Catholic Diocese of Aba, Senior Associate Editor-in-Chief, Hope International Magazine, 2008 till date.

HIS FIRST PUBLISHED ARTICLE

His first published article was titled, *Sainthood: You can also make it,* written in his first year philosophy in Bigard, 1992 and published in Torch Magazine. The publication deeply spurred him and since then, he has inspired many through his other published articles, biographies, tributes and poems. He has also helped to proof-read books, academic thesis and articles for people. This is actually his first published book.

SECRETARY

He has been appointed and has served as secretary in many groups and organizations. Secretary, St. Paul's Catholic Church Choir, Umuode Nsulu, 1993/1995; Secretary, Our Lady Mirror of Justice Praesidium, St. Joseph's Parish, Kirikiri Apapa Lagos, 1997/1998; Secretary, Umunna Post-Secondary Students Association,1989/1990; Secretary, Aba Diocesan Seminarians Association; Bigard Enugu, 1994/1996;

Secretary-General, Nigerian Federation of Catholic Students, Bigard Enugu Chapter, 1999/200; Secretary, UmuodeUSA, June 2008 till date. As a theology student in Bigard, he held the post of Vice President of NACATHS (National Association of Catholic Theology Students), 2000/2001. These responsibilities have taken him to many places for meetings and conferences.

APOSTOLIC WORK AS SEMINARIAN

As a senior seminarian, he did his Apostolic Work in the following parishes: St.Odilia Osokwa, 1993; St. Jude Orhuru, 1994; Regina Caeli Obehie, 1995; SS Peter & Paul Mbutungwa, 1996; Annunciation Seminary Amaudara (Auxiliary teacher), 1997; St. John Iheorji, 1998; St. Martin Abagana, Awka Diocese (Inter-Diocese), 1999; St. Margaret Umuokporji, 2000; He was ordained a Deacon on December 16, 2000; St. John Iheorji, 2001, (Holy Week/Easter Assingment).

DEVOTION TO THE BLESSED VIRGIN MARY

He is a devotee to the Blessed Virgin Mary. Before and during his formation in Bigard, he was and still is a member of the Legion of Mary Society. He was the treasurer of his praesidium, Mother of the Church in 1998. In 1999 he was made the vice president and in 2000 he became the president. He was also a member of Pioneer Association of Total Abstinence from alcohol.

ACTOR/DRAMA STUDENT

He was a member of Bigard Theatre Group, and this offered him opportunities to act on stage as a woman, boy, old man etc. His involvement in Bigard Theatre Group among other things, helped him to conquer stage fright and deeply improved his eloquence, public-speaking and self-confidence.

HIS ELOQUENCE AND PUBLIC SPEAKING

Owing to his ready wit, eloquence and motivational speaking, he was asked several times by the Bigard Memorial Seminary Authorities to render a speech "Vote of Thanks" on behalf of the Staff and Students during official visits of Governors, Bishops, Papal Authorities or any dignitary to the seminary. He was well known in his seminary days for blending some of those public speeches with Latin dictums which really resonated with his listeners.

He had been asked to be the MC (Master of Ceremony), preacher or spokesman of his group at different public ceremonies such as, First Mass of newly ordained priests, concerts and or Aba presbyterial gatherings.

While in the Bishop's court, Christ the King Cathedral Aba, (2001/2006), he was given the privilege a few times by the Bishop to give "Vote of Thanks" on behalf of the house to dignitaries at special occasions.

Even when sometimes taken on the spot, he had most times proved his mettle having managed public ceremonies for years. At such times, he shares some of the proverbs he learnt from his grand-father and they most often sold the message. To beef-up this skill, he has done extensive private research and studies on public/motivational speaking.

MERIT AWARDS

In recognition and appreciation of his creative writings and sacred eloquence, the Rotary Club of Nigeria, Ogbor Hill Aba Chapter gave him a Merit Award in 2003 and the Faculty of Law, Abia State University Uturu also gave him a Merit Award in 2005. These Awards bear glaring witness to the positive impact his pastoral ministry and creative writings have made and still makes in peoples' lives.

NATIONAL WORKSHOPS

With the permission and help of his Bishop, he participated in the following National Workshops: National Workshop for Communications Directors and Editors of Catholic Newspapers, Reatreat Pastoral Centre Okpunor, Awka Diocese, August 2001; National Workshop for Communications Directors and Editors of Catholic Newspapers, Catholic Institute of West Africa, Port Harcourt,

2002; National Workshop for Nigerian Mass Communicators, Civic Centre, University of Ibadan, 2003. He earned Merit Certificates at the end of each of these workshops.

SOCIAL LIFE

Father Peter is a joyful person. He has great passion for reading, writing, charity, laughter and sharing experiences and pleasantries with people. He loves listening to and spending time with elderly people. His closeness to his grand-mother and grand-father helped to prepare him for this way of life.

INTEREST IN MUSIC/SINGING

In his theology years in the seminary, he was a member of the Bigard Main Choir. He loves songs and music and always encouraged people to sing at Mass. He sometimes uses songs to spice up his sermons. This deeply edifies him. He believes that music is one of the channels through which we dispose God's mind to listen to us and answer our prayers.

MODEL SAINT

His model saint is St. Philip who is well known for his joyful spirit. He has the notion that everybody is important to God therefore, everybody deserves to be loved. This conviction is the driving-force of his priestly ministry.

MOTTO

His motto is, *Servire in Laetitia*, (Latin) meaning, *To Serve in Joy*. He borrowed this from his Bishop, Most Rev. V.V. Ezeonyia, CSSP whose motto is exactly, *"Servire in Laetitia"*.

BOOKS

Of all the books he has read, the ones that made the profoundest impressions on him are: *The Bible, Become a Better You,* by Joel Osteen and *The Shark,* by WM. Paul Young.

—Rev. Fr. Polycarp Okechukwu Ochieze.
Pastor, St. Peter's Parish Ohuhu Nsulu,
Isiala Ngwa North LGA, Abia State, Nigeria.

REFERENCES

1. *http://www.answers.com/topic/humility.*

2. *http://en.wikipedia.org/wiki/Five_Virtues.*

3. *http://www.quatationspage.com/subjects/humility.*

4. *http://encouragingbiblequotes.com/versespridea.html.*

5. *http://www.bibleinsong.com/Promises/Duties_man/Humility/ Humility.htm.*

6. *http://www.tentmaker.org/Quotes/humilityquotesl.htm.*

7. *http://www.pietyhilldesign.com/gcq/quotepages/humility.ht.mlh.*

8. *http://www.finequotes.com/select_quote-category-Humility—page-0.htm.*

9. *http://www.finequotes.com/select_quote-category-Humility-page-1.htm.*

10. *http://www.finequotes.com/select_quote-category-Humility-page-3.htm.*

11. *http://www.finequotes.com/select_quote.category-Humility-page-3.htm.*

12. *http://www.brainyquote.com/quotes/quotes/t/thomassmo282773.html.*

13. *http://www.brainyquote.com/quotes/quotes/d/davidmalle204308.htm.*

14. *http://www.brainyquote.com/quotes/quotes/a/alphonsus1358205.htm.*

15. *http://www.brainyquote.com/quotes/quotes/c/cslewis115356.html.*

16. *http://www.brainyquote.com/quotes/quotes/b/billyjacks405101.html.*

17. *http://www.gigausa.com/quotes/topics/humility_t001.htm.*

18. *http://www.leadershipnow.com/humilityquotes.html.*

19. *http://www.notablequotes.com/h/humility_quotes.html*

20. *http://wisdomquotes.com/cat_humility.html.*

21. *http://mikeratliff.wordpress.com/2007/11/10/humility-the-mark-of-a-genuine-disciple/.*

22. *http://www.inspirationpeak.com/cgibin/search.cgi?search=character.*

23. *http://www.inspirationpeak.com/cgibin/search.cgi?search=Mahatma+Gandhi&page+1.*

24. *http://www.gigausa.com/quotes/topics/meekness_t001.htm.*

25. *http://christianresearchnetwork.com/?p+3694.*

26. *http://www.enduringword.com/commentaries/0926.htm.*

27. *http://www.ucgstp.org/lit/vt/vt/08/king.htm.*